the TUDORS

by Alice Proctor
Consultant: Alison Howard

How to use this book

Each topic in this book is clearly labelled and contains all these components:

Topic heading

Introduction to the topic

Sub-topic 1 offers complete information about one aspect of the topic

Words in capitals are explained in the Glossary

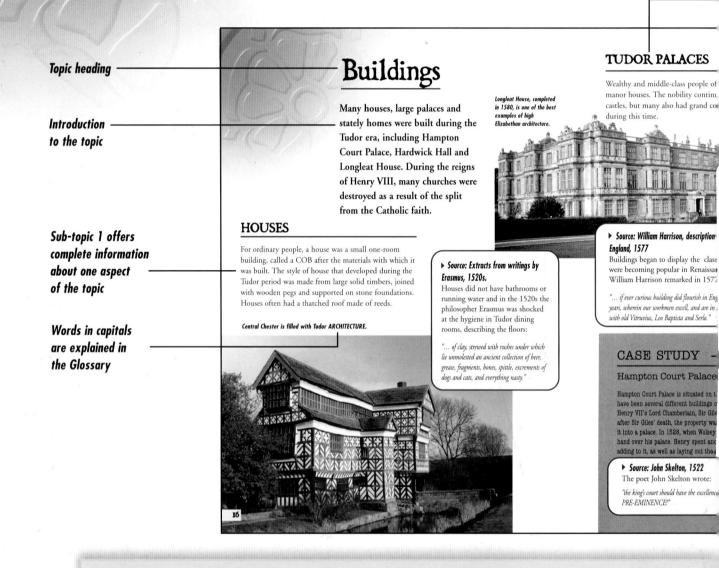

Buildings

Many houses, large palaces and stately homes were built during the Tudor era, including Hampton Court Palace, Hardwick Hall and Longleat House. During the reigns of Henry VIII, many churches were destroyed as a result of the split from the Catholic faith.

HOUSES

For ordinary people, a house was a small one-room building, called a COB after the materials with which it was built. The style of house that developed during the Tudor period was made from large solid timbers, joined with wooden pegs and supported on stone foundations. Houses often had a thatched roof made of reeds.

Central Chester is filled with Tudor ARCHITECTURE.

Longleat House, completed in 1580, is one of the best examples of high Elizabethan architecture.

▶ **Source: Extracts from writings by Erasmus, 1520s.**
Houses did not have bathrooms or running water and in the 1520s the philosopher Erasmus was shocked at the hygiene in Tudor dining rooms, describing the floors:

"... of clay, strewed with rushes under which lie unmolested an ancient collection of beer, grease, fragments, bones, spittle, excrements of dogs and cats, and everything nasty."

TUDOR PALACES

Wealthy and middle-class people of manor houses. The nobility continu castles, but many also had grand co during this time.

▶ **Source: William Harrison, description England, 1577**
Buildings began to display the class were becoming popular in Renaissa William Harrison remarked in 1577

"... if ever curious building did flourish in Eng years, wherein our workmen excell, and are in with old Vitruvius, Leo Baptista and Serlo."

CASE STUDY —

Hampton Court Palace

Hampton Court Palace is situated on t have been several different buildings o Henry VII's Lord Chamberlain, Sir Gile after Sir Giles' death, the property wa it into a palace. In 1528, when Wolsey hand over his palace. Henry spent and adding to it, as well as laying out tha-

▶ **Source: John Skelton, 1522**
The poet John Skelton wrote:

"the king's court should have the excellence PRE-EMINENCE!"

16

ISBN 978 1 84898 075 4

This edition published in 2009 by *ticktock* Media Ltd

Printed in China

9 8 7 6 5 4 3 2 1

A CIP catalogue record for this book is available from the British Library.

Copyright © *ticktock* Entertainment Ltd 2005. First published in Great Britain in 2005 by *ticktock* Media Ltd, The Old Sawmill, 103 Goods Station Road, Tunbridge Wells, Kent, TN1 2DP.

Sub-topic 2 offers complete information about one aspect of the topic

Some suggested words to use in your project

Words to use in your project

chimney pot – a short pipe fitted to a chimney to help smoke escape
daub – to cover or smear with plaster or grease
estate – a large property with grounds; land
memorial – a monument
sceptre – a ceremonial staff held by a king or queen

The Glossary explains the meaning of any unusual or difficult words appearing on these two pages

Glossary

architecture – the art of designing and constructing buildings
cob – a mixture of compressed clay and straw
pre-eminence – the state of being better than all others

Other pages in the book that relate to what you have read are listed in this bar

See also: The Tudor Monarchs 6–7; Art 20–21; Tudor Towns 28–29

The Case Study is a closer look at a famous person, artefact or building that relates to the topic

Captions clearly explain what is in the picture

Each photo or illustration is described and discussed in its accompanying text

CONTENTS

THE TUDORS   4–5

THE TUDOR MONARCHS   6–7

MARRIAGE AND FAMILY   8–9

RELIGION   10–11

CLOTHES AND JEWELLERY   12–13

SIGNIFICANT PEOPLE   14–15

BUILDINGS   16–17

THEATRE   18–19

ART   20–21

FOOD AND DRINK   22–23

CRIME AND PUNISHMENT   24–25

REBELLIONS   26–27

TUDOR TOWNS   28–29

SPORTS AND PASTIMES   30–31

INDEX AND TIMELINE   32

The Tudors

The Tudors were a family that ruled England from 1485 to 1603. Henry VII became the first Tudor king when he defeated Richard III of York in 1485. This ended the 30-year CONFLICT called the Wars of the Roses. Henry VII married Elizabeth of York to unite the two FEUDING sides. The Tudor DYNASTY produced the famous monarchs Henry VIII and Elizabeth I.

THE RISE OF THE TUDORS

When Henry VII came to the throne, he had to restore peace and stability. He stopped members of the nobility overthrowing him by DISBANDING their private armies and taking their wealth. Soon he was strong enough to prevent a revolt. The king acquired the moral support of the people of England. By the time of his death in 1509, England was the most prosperous and stable it had been for 50 years.

> ▶ **Source: *The obituary of King Henry VII, Anglica Historia, 1509***
> The obituary of Henry VII gives us an idea of his power:
>
> *"He well knew how to maintain his royal majesty and all which APPERTAINS to kingship at every time and in every place."*

This is a portrait of Henry VII clutching the red rose of the House of Lancaster.

TUDOR ROLES

The social structure of Tudor England was HIERARCHICAL. The king was head of England and the Royal Court existed to serve him.

Ordinary people worked the land and sold excess produce to market.

> ▶ **Source: Edward Hall, 'The CORONATIONS of Henry VIII and Catherine of Aragon', 1509**
>
> An account of the coronations of Henry VIII and Catherine of Aragon:
>
> *"According to sacred tradition and ancient custom, his grace and the queen were anointed and crowned by the ARCHBISHOP of Canterbury in the presence of other PRELATES of the realm and the nobility and a large number of civic DIGNITARIES."*

Society was divided into different classes. Lords at the Royal Court and religious leaders held important positions. Ordinary people ranged from peasants to businessmen and merchants.

Words to use in your project

ambivalent – *unable to make a decision*
ancestry – *family descent*
besiege – *to surround with armed forces*
campaign – *operation, crusade, drive, warfare*
legitimacy – *fairness, lawfulness, legality*
tainted – *corrupted*
triumphal – *in celebration*

Glossary

appertains – *relates to; concerns*
archbishop – *a bishop of the highest rank who presides over an archbishopric or archdiocese*
conflict – *a fight, disagreement*
coronations – *ceremonies to crown a king or queen*
dignitaries – *important people*
disbanding – *breaking up*
dynasty – *a succession of rulers belonging to the same family*
feuding – *quarrelling*
hierarchical – *arranged in order of rank*
prelates – *bishops or other clergy*

See also: Marriage and Family 8–9; Religion 10–11; Tudor Towns 28–29

CASE STUDY

The Wars of the Roses

For 30 years from 1455, two families fought over who was to be king of England. The House of Lancaster, the symbol of which was a red rose, was led by Henry Tudor, while Richard III led the House of York, known by its white rose. On 22 August 1485, the two armies met near Bosworth, Leicestershire.

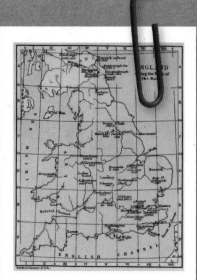

A map showing the main battlefields of the Wars of the Roses.

> ▶ **Source: Croyland Chronicle, 1485**
>
> This excerpt describes the death of Richard III:
>
> *"King Richard ... received many mortal wounds, and like a spirited and most courageous prince, fell in the battle and not in flight."*

The Tudor Monarchs

The Tudor DYNASTY began with Henry VII. In 1509 he died and his son Henry became king. Henry's only son, Edward VI, was king from 1547–53. As he was dying, Edward was persuaded to name a distant relative, Lady Jane Grey, as his successor. Jane was queen for nine days, until Edward's sister Mary DEPOSED her. Mary Tudor reigned from 1553–58. The last Tudor was Elizabeth I.

HENRY VIII

Henry VIII ruled from 1509 to 1547 and is probably the most famous Tudor MONARCH. He was originally destined to be the archbishop of Canterbury until Prince Arthur, his elder brother, died in 1502. Just 18 when he became king, the English people loved him at first, especially those who had been heavily taxed by his father.

Henry's 38-year REIGN was eventful. He spent much of the money his father saved on his extravagant lifestyle. He broke from the Catholic faith and created the new Protestant Church of England in 1533, causing conflict within England and with many of the Catholic countries in Europe. In England he called for the monasteries and convents to be destroyed, and was the first English king to have a permanent navy.

> ▶ **Source: A contemporary description of King Henry VIII written by the Venetian AMBASSADOR to his court, 1515**
>
> *"His Majesty is the handsomest POTENTATE I ever set eyes on … He speaks French, English, and Latin, and a little Italian, plays well on the lute and harpsichord …"*

This portrait of Henry VIII was painted in 1536 by Hans Holbein the Younger.

ELIZABETH I

Elizabeth I's reign is often called the Golden Age. England became powerful within Europe and trade, the arts and culture flourished.

▶ **Source: Elizabeth's speech at Tilbury, 1588**

In 1588, Elizabeth gave this speech to troops gathered to fight the Spanish Armada:

> "… I know I have the body but of a weak and feeble woman; but I have the heart and stomach of a king, and of a king of England too."

Elizabeth never married, so on her death the Tudor dynasty came to an end.

This picture shows Elizabeth I at her coronation in 1558.

Words to use in your project

absolute power – *complete authority*
beheading – *a form of execution where the head is cut off*
expeditions – *voyages*
golden age – *an ideal and prosperous period*
Reformation – *a 16th-century Protestant movement*
successor – *an heir to the throne*

Glossary

ambassador – *the highest-ranking representative of a country*
divorced – *to be formally released from a marriage*
deposed – *removed*
dynasty – *a succession of rulers belonging to the same family*
heir – *a person entitled to inherit property*
monarch – *a ruler of a nation*
potentate – *a monarch or ruler*
reign – *a period of rule*

See also: The Tudors 4–5; Art 20–21; Crime and Punishment 24–25; Sports and Pastimes 30–31

CASE STUDY

Henry VIII's six wives

Henry VIII's first wife, Catherine of Aragon, was the mother of Mary I, but in 1533 Henry DIVORCED her. His next wife, Anne Boleyn, gave birth to his daughter Elizabeth but was beheaded in 1536. Jane Seymour, Henry's third wife, produced his HEIR, Edward, but he died shortly afterwards. Henry's final three wives were Anne of Cleves (whom he divorced), Catherine Howard (whom was beheaded) and Catherine Parr (whom outlived him).

▶ **Source: Letter from Anne Boleyn to Henry VIII, 1526**

This excerpt is from a letter from Anne Boleyn to Henry:

"… I am Your Majesty's very obliged and very obedient servant, without any reserve."

This is a portrait of Anne Boleyn in her mid-twenties.

Marriage and Family

In Tudor times people often lived in extended families, so as well as parents and children, there might be widowed aunts or grandparents living in the same house. Life expectancy was low and most people did not live beyond the age of 40. The legal age for marriage was 14 for boys and 12 for girls and the idea of marrying for love was thought foolish.

WEDDING CUSTOMS

The public reading of the BANNS in the local parish on three consecutive Sundays showed that a couple intended to be married. The wedding was a religious ceremony conducted by a minister. Wedding rings were not exchanged, but some rings were engraved with a posy – a short poem.

▶ **Source: Engraving on 16th–17th century gold ring at The British Museum, London, England**
This posy is engraved on a Tudor-era ring:

"Many are thee starrs I see yet in my eye no starr like thee."

This picture shows Elizabeth I at the wedding of her maid of honour, Anne Russell, in 1600.

HEIRS AND INHERITANCE

Property, titles and money were very important in Tudor society, and the eldest son was the legal HEIR. A girl with no brothers could inherit her father's property. When a girl from a wealthy family married, a DOWRY would be paid by her father.

Henry VIII's brother, Prince Arthur, was heir to the throne, but died.

▶ **Source: Richard Grafton, an account of the death of Prince Arthur, 1569**

Henry VIII had to wait a month before he could be named heir to the throne. If his brother's wife had been pregnant, the child would have become heir:

"After his (Prince Arthur's) death the name of prince belonged to his brother the duke of York, since his brother died without issue ... But the duke, suspecting that his brother's wife was with child ... was by a month or more delayed from his title, name and PRE-EMINENCE."

Words to use in your project

admonition – *a warning*
apostasy – *the abandonment of a belief or principle*
exemplary – *the best of its kind*
heresy – *an opinion opposed to official or established views or doctrines*
posthumous – *after death*
registry – *a place where official records are kept*

Glossary

banns – *a notice read out, announcing an intended marriage*
dowry – *the property or money brought by a bride to her husband on their marriage*
heir – *a person entitled to inherit property*
morsels – *bite-sized pieces of food*
pottage – *a soup or stew*
pre-eminence – *better than all others*

See also: The Tudor Monarchs 6–7; Buildings 16–17; Rebellions 26–27

CASE STUDY

A child's life

In Tudor times, half the babies born died before their first birthday – from disease or poor living conditions. Children were treated like small adults and discipline was strict. Only privileged boys and girls were given an education.

▶ **Source: Hugh Rhodes, The Boke of Nurture, 1577**

Manners were important, as this excerpt from a 16th-century book shows:

"At dinner, press not thyself too high; sit in the place appointed thee. Sup not loud of thy POTTAGE ... Eat small MORSELS of meat; eat softly, and drink mannerly."

Naming a baby was an important family event.

Religion

During the reign of Henry VII, most people in England were CATHOLIC, which meant the Pope could overrule the king. The Pope would not let Henry divorce his first wife, Catherine of Aragon. Henry broke away from the Pope's control and named himself head of a new Church of England.

PROTEST AND CHANGE

The period of religious change across Europe is called the Reformation. People criticized the behaviour of priests and protested against the Pope's authority.

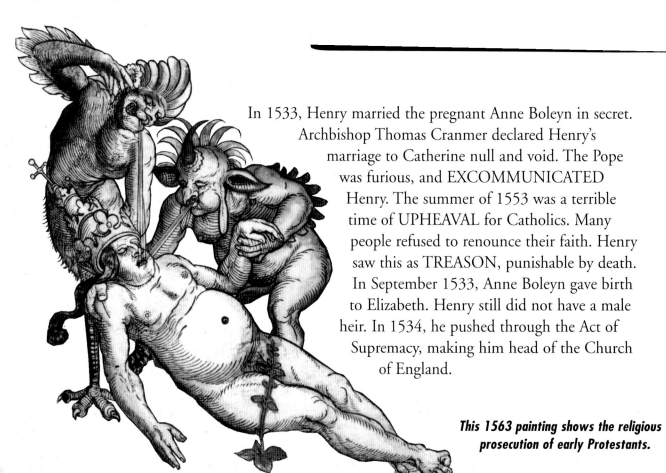

In 1533, Henry married the pregnant Anne Boleyn in secret. Archbishop Thomas Cranmer declared Henry's marriage to Catherine null and void. The Pope was furious, and EXCOMMUNICATED Henry. The summer of 1553 was a terrible time of UPHEAVAL for Catholics. Many people refused to renounce their faith. Henry saw this as TREASON, punishable by death. In September 1533, Anne Boleyn gave birth to Elizabeth. Henry still did not have a male heir. In 1534, he pushed through the Act of Supremacy, making him head of the Church of England.

This 1563 painting shows the religious prosecution of early Protestants.

THE ENGLISH REFORMATION

It was not until the reign of Elizabeth I that England truly became a PROTESTANT nation. During the reign of Edward V, Acts of Parliament were passed that demanded that everyone should become Protestant. When Edward's Catholic sister Mary came to the throne, she REINSTATED the Catholic Church. Elizabeth I had to tread very carefully to unite England.

▶ **Source: Speech to Parliament by Elizabeth 1, 1558**

This is Elizabeth's speech to parliament:

"… now that the publick Care of governing the Kingdom is laid upon me … I have already joyned my self in Marriage to an Husband, namely, the Kingdom of England."

During the Reformation, most church decorations were removed.

Words to use in your project

contemplation – *the act of religious or mystical meditation*
inferior – *lower in quality*
monastic – *relating to monks and monasteries*
paradox – *a statement that sounds odd but might prove true*
salvation – *a deliverance from sin*
spire – *a steeple, cone, pinnacle*

Glossary

Catholic – *a member of a Christian religion with the Pope as its head*
excommunicated – *excluded from the Christian Church*
monasteries – *places where monks live*
Protestant – *a member of a Christian religion that does not acknowledge the Pope as its head*
reinstated – *restored to a former condition or position*
treason – *treachery, disloyalty; betraying or attempting to overthrow the government*
upheaval – *a sudden, violent change*

See also: Marriage and Family 8–9; Buildings 16–17; Art 20–21; Crime and Punishment 24–25

CASE STUDY

Monasteries

In Tudor times, powerful MONASTERIES the cultivated land in England. Ho seemed to be slipping, so Hen

…port on a monastery in Lincoln, 1518

…Cromwell's report said:

…he prior is frequently drunk … The brothers of the monastery, especially the older ones, play dice and other games for money."

In 1535, Henry VIII ordered 376 monaste Between 1536 and 1540 he sold for himself.

The ruins of Castle Acre Priory, which was surrendered to Henry VIII in 1537.

Clothes and Jewellery

During the Tudor period, clothing styles changed dramatically. Strict SUMPTUARY laws regulated what fabrics could be used and ensured people dressed according to their class. FASHION was also influenced by the rest of Europe and the East.

WHAT THEY WORE

In early Tudor times, women wore floor-length dresses with a tight-fitting bodice and a square neckline. Men wore a shirt and stockings, with a DOUBLET over the top. Working men might wear BREECHES and a TUNIC.

The Peasant Dance, *painted in 1568 by Pieter Breugel the Elder. Displayed in Kunsthistorisches Museum, Vienna, Austria.*

▶ **Source: Sumptuary law of Tudor England**

A law was passed to stop ordinary people dressing like nobles. The punishment for disobeying these Sumptuary laws could be a fine or even death. For men, the laws stated:

"None shall wear … cloth of gold or silver, or silk of purple colour … except Earls, all above that rank, and Knights of the King."

For women, the laws stated:

"None shall wear … silk or cloth mixed with or embroidered with silk, pearls, gold or silver … except … Baronesses and all above that rank."

TUDOR FASHION

It became fashionable for men to wear short trunks with knee-length breeches and a padded tunic. A ruff vas worn round the neck and at the cuffs. Both boys nd girls up to the age of six wore dresses. Increasing ade in fine cloths meant that people could show eir wealth through fashion.

> ▶ **Source: Philip Stubbes, The Anatomie of Abuses, from The Second Tome of Homilies, 1583**
>
> Puritan Phillip Stubbes spoke out against the importance people placed on clothing in a 1583 sermon:
>
> *"As these gownes be of DIVERS and SUNDRIES colours, so are they of divers fashions, changing with the Moon, for some be of the new fashion, some of the olde, some of this fashion, and some of that …"*

Clothes worn by royal men.

Words to use in your project

brocade – *a rich fabric with a raised pattern*

cloth of gold – *cloth woven from threads of real gold with silk or wool*

corsets – *tight undergarments worn by both women and men to shape the figure*

hose – *stockings*

mantle – *a type of cloak*

unguent – *an ointment or lotion, often scented*

Glossary

breeches – *short trousers fastened just below the knee*

divers – *varying types of*

doublet – *a short padded jacket*

fashion – *a popular trend or style*

linen – *a type of light fabric*

sumptuary – *relating to laws that regulate expense or extravagance*

sundries – *various kinds*

tunic – *a loose, thigh-length garment*

See also: Marriage and Family 8–9; Theatre 18–19; Art 20–21

C

Queen Elizabeth I was famous for her ghostly complexion.

▶ **Source: Philip Stubbes, The Anatomie of Abuses, 1583**

Again, Stubbes had a view on how women used make-up:

"… to colour their faces with certain oyles, liquors, unguents and waters made to that end, whereby they think their beautie is greatly decored."

Significant People

Many great men of the Tudor period contributed to EXPLORATION, religion, art and literature. Henry VIII encouraged artists and intellectuals from Europe to be part of his court and to introduce it to new ideas.

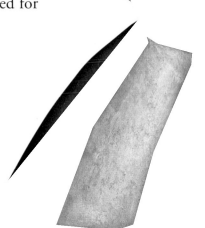

Thomas Wolsey was Lord Chancellor of England.

GREAT MEN

Thomas Wolsey served Henry VII and Henry VIII. When Henry VIII wanted to end his marriage to Catherine of Aragon, Wolsey's loyalties were divided and he eventually fell from favour. He was arrested for high TREASON, but died on his way to London in 1530.

> ▶ **Source: William Shakespeare, King Henry VIII, 1613**
>
> In Shakespeare's *King Henry VIII*, Catherine of Aragon describes Wolsey:
>
> *"He was a man of an unbounded stomach, ever ranking himself with princes ... but his performance, as he is now, nothing ..."*

Sir Walter Raleigh was a great adventurer whose military achievements and charm brought him to Elizabeth I's attention. She later imprisoned him for falling in love with one of her maids of honour. He was released, but when Elizabeth died, his enemies turned James I against him. He was beheaded. At his EXECUTION he asked to see the axe and said:

"This is a sharp Medicine, but it is a Physician for all Diseases."

FAMOUS CITIZENS

STATESMAN Thomas Cromwell became Henry VIII's adviser after Wolsey's death. Cromwell persuaded Henry to marry Anne of Cleves, which was a disaster. Henry executed him in 1540 for treason. SCHOLAR and intellectual Sir Thomas More could not accept Henry as head of the Church of England, so he resigned from his job of Lord Chancellor. He was tried for treason and executed.

> ### ▶ Source: Henry VIII's Attorney-General at the trial of Sir Thomas More, 1535
>
> At his trial, the Attorney-General said:
>
> *"Even though we should have no word or deed to charge upon you, yet we have your silence, and that is a sign of your evil intention and a sure proof of malice."*

Thomas More with his family.

Words to use in your project

ecstatic – *elated, overjoyed*
exultant – *jubilant*
indignant – *displeased by unfair treatment*
jurisdiction – *the authority to make laws*
polemic – *a verbal or written debate*
recant – *to renounce in a formal or public way*
scrupulous – *extremely careful*

Glossary

circumnavigate – *to sail all the way around*
execution – *the act of putting to death*
expedition – *a journey with a definite objective*
exploration – *the act of travelling to and studying unfamiliar areas*
scholar – *a person who is highly educated and knowledgeable*
statesman – *a respected political figure*
treason – *treachery, disloyalty; betraying or attempting to overthrow the government*

See also: The Tudors 4–5; Religion 10–11; Tudor Towns 28–29; Art 20–21; Crime and Punishment 24-25; Rebellions 26–27

CASE STUDY

Sir Francis D...

Sir Francis Drake ...
CIRCUMNAVIG...
returned th...
achieved great fame and victory against ...

> ### ▶ Source: Inscription Armada medal issued by Elizabeth I to Sir Francis Drake in 1588
>
> Elizabeth I gave Drake a medal with these words inscribed on it:
>
> *"God blew with His wind, and they were scattered."*
>
> Drake died in 1596 in the West Indies, on an EXPEDITION against the Spanish.

Statue of Sir Francis Drake.

Buildings

Many houses, large palaces and stately homes were built during the Tudor era, including Hampton Court Palace, Hardwick Hall and Longleat House. During the reign of Henry VIII, many churches were destroyed as a result of the split from the Catholic faith.

Longleat House, completed in 1580, is one of the best examples of high Elizabethan architecture.

HOUSES

For ordinary people, a house was a small one-room building, called a COB after the materials with which it was built. The style of house that developed during the Tudor period was made from large solid timbers, joined with wooden pegs and supported on stone foundations. Houses often had a thatched roof made of reeds.

Central Chester is filled with Tudor ARCHITECTURE.

▶ Source: Extracts from writings by Erasmus, 1520s

Houses did not have bathrooms or running water and in the 1520s the philosopher Erasmus was shocked at the hygiene in Tudor dining rooms. He described the floors:

"… of clay, strewed with rushes under which lie unmolested an ancient collection of beer, grease, fragments, bones, spittle, excrements of dogs and cats, and everything nasty."

TUDOR PALACES

Wealthy and middle-class people often lived in small manor houses. The nobility continued to live in their castles, but many also had grand country houses built during this time.

> ▶ **Source: William Harrison, description of Elizabethan England, 1577**
>
> Buildings began to display the classical shapes that were becoming popular in Renaissance Europe, as William Harrison remarked in 1577:
>
> *"… if ever curious building did flourish in England, it is in these our years, wherein our workmen excell, and are in a manner comparable with old Vitruvius, Leo Baptista and Serlo."*

Words to use in your project

chimney pot – *a short pipe fitted to a chimney to help smoke escape*

daub – *to cover or smear with plaster or grease*

estate – *a large property with grounds; land*

memorial – *a monument*

sceptre – *a ceremonial staff held by a king or queen*

Glossary

architecture – *the art of designing and constructing buildings*

cob – *a mixture of compressed clay and straw*

pre-eminence – *the state of being better than all others*

See also: The Tudor Monarchs 6–7; Art 20–21; Tudor Towns 28–29

CASE STUDY

Hampton Court Palace

Hampton Court Palace is situated on the River Thames in London. There have been several different buildings on the site, including the home of Henry VII's Lord Chamberlain, Sir Giles Daubeney. In 1514, six years after Sir Giles' death, the property was given to Thomas Wolsey, who built it into a palace. In 1528, when Wolsey fell from favour, he was forced to hand over his palace. Henry spent another ten years rebuilding and adding to it, as well as laying out the plan for the now famous gardens.

> ▶ **Source: John Skelton, 1522**
>
> The poet John Skelton wrote:
>
> *"the king's court should have the excellence … But Hampton Court hath PRE-EMINENCE!"*

The west front of Hampton Court as it is today.

Theatre

During the Tudor period, theatres started to be built. Traditionally, travelling actors and musicians had gone from town to town performing plays. After a while there were fears these actors might be spreading the PLAGUE. In 1572, travelling actors were banned, and Elizabeth I allowed four noblemen to start their own theatre companies.

DRAMAS, COSTUMES AND SETS

A PLAYHOUSE was like an AMPITHEATRE, where the audience sat around a central stage. Wealthy people sat in the GALLERY, while poorer people stood in the 'pit' in front of the stage. The most popular Elizabethan plays were comedies, tragedies, historical plays and love stories. PROPS and costumes helped the audience work out the characters' status or profession. But if actors wore their costumes in the streets, high-class people complained, saying it flouted the Sumptuary laws.

▶ **Source: Stephen Gosson, The School of Abuse, 1579**
In 1579, Stephen Gosson wrote:

"... the very hyrelings ... under gentlemen's noses in sutes of silke ... look askance over the shoulder at every man, of whom the Sunday before they begged an almes."

Elizabethan travelling performers, in elaborate costumes.

SHAKESPEARE AND OTHERS

The most famous PLAYWRIGHT was William Shakespeare, born in Stratford-upon-Avon in 1564. By 1592 he had begun to make a name for himself as both an actor and a playwright. His real fame came after he joined a theatre company called the Lord Chamberlain's Men in 1594. He began to perform for Elizabeth I, and to write plays such as *Richard III*.

This portrait of Shakespeare was painted in 1603.

> ▶ **Source: William Shakespeare, Richard III, 1597**
>
> *"Thou offspring of the house of Lancaster The wronged heirs of York do pray for thee Good angels guard thy battle! live, and flourish!"*
> Other writers of the time include Francis Beaumont, Christopher Marlowe, Philip Massinger and John Webster.

Words to use in your project

comedy – *a pleasant or humorous play with a happy ending*
disguise – *to hide or obscure*
majestic – *having or characterized by dignity and power*
tragedy – *a serious play dealing with tragic events and having an unhappy ending*

Glossary

amphitheatre – *a circular building with an open space surrounded by rising rows of seats*
gallery – *the highest balcony in a theatre, with the cheapest seats*
plague – *a contagious disease that spreads quickly*
playhouse – *a theatre for live dramatic productions*
playwright – *the author of a play*
props – *the portable objects used in a play*

See also: Clothes and Jewellery 12–13; Significant People 14–15; Art 20–21

CASE STUDY

The Globe Theatre

The Lord Chamberlain's Men played at one of two theatres in Blackfriars, London. When the lease on the land ran out, the Lord Chamberlain's Men dismantled the theatre, using the materials to construct the Globe Theatre on the south bank of the Thames. It burned down in 1613 when a cannon was accidentally shot into its roof during Shakespeare's Henry VIII. The Globe Theatre has now been rebuilt on its original site.

> ▶ **Source: William Shakespeare, The Tempest, 1611**
>
> This line from Shakespeare's play *The Tempest* seems to refer to it:
>
> *"The cloud capp'd towers, the gorgeous palaces, the solemn temples, the great globe itself."*

The Globe Theatre today.

Art

The arts flourished under the Tudors, whose reign coincided with the Renaissance that swept across Europe, changing the style of music, painting, sculpture and architecture. Henry VII was a PATRON of the arts who encouraged Italian and French artists and philosophers to visit England.

PAINTING

Henry VIII introduced the idea of painting royal family portraits. When English artists did not impress him, he looked to Flemish, German and Italian painters. The most notable of these was the German artist Hans Holbein, whose paintings gave new life to the portraits of Henry VIII and his court.

> ▶ **Source: Letter of introduction from Erasmus to his friends in England, 1526**
> Erasmus commented on Holbein's popularity:
>
> *"… here the arts are freezing, so Holbein is on the way to England to pick up some coins there."*

By 1537, Holbein was Henry's court painter. His works give a VIVID picture of the Tudor court. When Elizabeth was on the throne, paintings of the monarch became increasingly elaborate. Many depicted images of power and majesty.

Self-portrait of Hans Holbein (1542–43) at the Galleria degli Uffizi in Florence, Italy.

WEAPONS AND ARMOUR

Tudor courts were often places of great music making and dancing, and many composers also wrote music for them. Famous composers and musicians include Thomas Byrd, Thomas Tallis and John Dowland. Henry VIII was a talented musician and composer, and is reputed to have written the popular English song 'Greensleeves'.

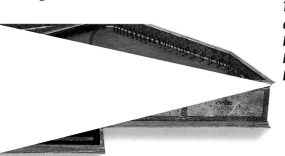

This GITTERN was a gift to Robert Dudley, Earl of Leicester, from Elizabeth I.

> ▶ **Source: Henry VIII manuscript, the source of most of the king's lyrical works, 1513**
>
> Many of his Henry's lyrics survive such as:
>
> *"Alas, what shall I do for love? For love, alas, what shall I do? Since now so kind I do you find To kepe you me unto. Alasse!"*
>
> Other Tudor kings and queens were skilled at the lute and Elizabeth I played the VIRGINAL.

Words to use in your project

chivalry – *the medieval system for knights with its strong moral code of behaviour*
courtiers – *the attendants at a royal court*
madrigal – *an unaccompanied song or short poem suitable for singing*
sketch – *a simple drawing done rapidly and with little detail*

Glossary

gittern – *a lute like medieval stringed instrument*
miniature – *very small*
patron – *a sponsor or supporter*
technique – *a method of procedure*
virginal – *a small rectangular harpsichord*
vivid – *bright; presenting a clear or strong picture*

See also: The Tudors 4–5; Clothes and Jewellery 12–13; Theatre 18–19; Tudor Towns 28–29

> ▶ **Source: Nicholas Hilliard, Arte of Limning, 1600**
>
> A favourite of Elizabeth I was Nicholas Hilliard, who u
> a special painting TECHNIQUE that Elizabeth liked:
>
> *"… for the lyne without shadows showeth all to good jugment, but the shadowe without lyne showeth nothing."*

This portrait of Elizabeth 1 was painted by Marcus Gheeraerts the Younger.

Food and Drink

In Tudor England, wealthy people tended to eat lots of meat, while ordinary people ate fruit and vegetables. Bread, butter and cheese were common, and as it was safer to drink than water, beer was the standard drink for children and adults.

MEAT AND BREAD

Rich people ate the meat of a wide range of animals including deer, boar, rabbits, sheep, cows, goats and pigs. They also ate fish and birds including peacocks, geese, pigeons, blackbirds and doves. Poor people could occasionally afford chicken, mutton and rabbit. The Tudors did not have much dietary knowledge, and rich people often suffered from SCURVY. Meat was often cooked with fruit, which made it taste sweet.

Only rich people could afford white bread, called manchet. The middle classes ate yeoman's bread, which was a darker colour and less expensive. Poorer people ate dark brown or black bread known as 'carter's bread'.

> ▶ Source: William Harrison, description of Elizabethan England, 1577
>
> This account describes the eating habits of Tudor people:
>
> "… there is no restraint of any meat either for religious sake or public order in England, but it is lawful for every man to feed upon whatsoever he is able to purchase."

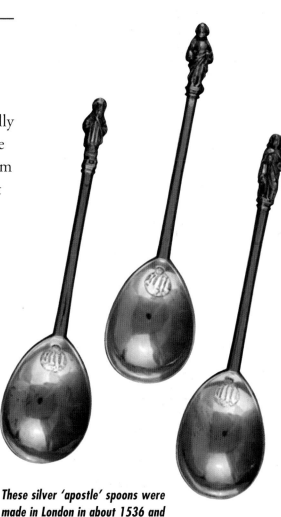

These silver 'apostle' spoons were made in London in about 1536 and would have been used by the GENTRY and wealthy merchants.

FEASTING

Tudor people celebrated special days, including Shrove Tuesday, Easter and Christmas, with feasts. Christmas puddings were made of meat, oatmeal and spices. Honey was used to sweeten foods and almond, cinnamon and clove were common flavourings.

This painting is called Feasting (Wedding at Bermondsey) by Joris Hoefnagel, 1569.

▶ **Source: George Wither, 'A Christmas Carol', 1633**

The spirit of feasting is illustrated in this poem by George Wither:

*"So now is come our joyful'st feast,
Let every man be jolly …
Drown sorrow in a cup of wine,
And let us all be merry."*

Words to use in your project

carnival – *a period of feasting and revelry, traditionally just before Lent*

cauldron – *a large metal pot with a lid and handle*

maritime – *of or relating to the sea, navigation and shipping*

staple – *a basic dietary item, such as flour, rice and corn*

Glossary

abroad – *in or to a foreign country or countries*

banquets – *ceremonial dinners*

gentry – *the class of people below the nobility in position and wealth*

imports – *goods or materials brought in from a foreign country*

scurvy – *a vitamin deficiency characterized by weakness and spongy gums*

tapioca – *a starchy, granular food used to make puddings*

See also: Sports and Pastimes 30–31

CASE STUDY

New foods

Many new foods came to Europe from the lands discovered by Tudor explorers. Maize (sweetcorn), potatoes, chocolate, peanuts, vanilla, tomatoes, pineapples, lima beans, peppers, TAPIOCA and turkey were all 'new' foods.

▶ **Source: William Harrison, description of Elizabethan England, 1577**
William Harrison lists these new IMPORTS:

"Of the potato, and such venerous roots as are brought out of … the Indies to furnish up our BANQUETS …"

Cocoa beans were introduced by explorer Christopher Columbus.

Oranges and other fruits imported from ABROAD were expensive and therefore only eaten by the rich.

Crime and Punishment

Tudor justice was very harsh. Heretics – people who had unorthodox religious beliefs – were burned at the stake. For nobles, being sent to the Tower of London meant imprisonment, perhaps torture and possibly death.

CRIME AND TORTURE

Crime during Tudor times fell into two categories: common crimes or capital offences. Common crimes included GOSSIPING too freely, cheating a customer and petty theft.

Common crimes were punished with a public whipping or time in the STOCKS.

Capital offences were crimes like MANSLAUGHTER, murder, highway robbery and witchcraft. Common people were hanged for these crimes and nobles beheaded.

The worst crime was treason – plotting to overthrow the government. Being found guilty of treason meant a gruesome death would follow.

▶ **Source: William Harrison description of Elizabethan England, 1577**

This was the sentence for John Fisher, found guilty of treason in 1535:

"John Fisher should … be drawn through the City of London to Tyburn, there to be hanged, cut down alive, his BOWELS taken out of his body and burnt before him, his head cut off, and his body be divided into four parts and his head and body be set in such places as the king should assign …"

This painting, called Macbeth's Justice, shows a public execution.

LAW AND COURTS

Henry VII passed reforms that created a central system that allowed appeals and an efficient local administration. He passed laws to protect poor people from injustice and give them free legal help. The important courts were the Quarter Sessions and the Court of Assizes.

This painting shows Sir William Cecil in the Court of Wards and Liveries.

▶ **Source: Excerpt from the diary of Swiss traveller Thomas Platter who came to London in 1599**

Thomas Platter gave an account of the workings of the law and courts:

"Especially every quarter when the law courts sit in London and they throng from all parts of England for the terms to litigate in numerous matters which have occurred in the interim, for everything is saved up till that time; then there is a slaughtering and a hanging …"

Words to use in your project

betray – to be disloyal to one's country, cause, etc.
decapitate – to cut off the head
gibbet – a structure from which bodies of criminals who had already been executed were hung

Glossary

bowels – the intestines
gossiping – the act of spreading rumours or talk of a personal or intimate nature
manslaughter – the unlawful killing of a human being by another wtithout being thought out beforehand
stocks – an instrument of punishment whereby a person's feet and hands are secured
unrest – a state of disturbance or disorder

See also: The Tudor Monarchs 6–7; Religion 10–11; Significant People 14–15; Rebellions 26–27

CASE STUDY

Justices of the Peace

Henry VII introduced new officers for the countryside, known as Justices of the Peace. These officers collected taxes, dealt with land disputes and awarded punishments. This system remained in effect until 1971.

▶ **Source: Thomas Berthel, The Boke for a Justyce of Peace, 1534**

This contemporary account says:

"Justices of peace should be good men and law full to determine felonies and trespasses committed and done agaynste the peace, and doo reasonable punyshement, accordyng to lawe and reason."

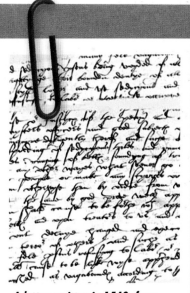

A letter, written in 1549, from King Edward VI to Justices of the Peace in counties where there had been UNREST.

Rebellions

There were many REBELLIONS in Tudor times. The Tudor monarchs were harsh on people who were involved in rebellions, and punishments were severe. REBELS were often publicly hanged to send a warning to others.

CAUSES OF REBELLION

Tudor monarchs gave people many reasons to rebel. Those from churches and monasteries revolted against King Henry VIII when he outlawed the Catholic Church. As farming methods changed and wool was in demand, the landowners needed fewer people to help them farm their land. This led to a 1549 peasant REVOLT in Norfolk, led by Robert Kett. Thousands of peasants ripped down the fences that had been put up to create sheep pastures.

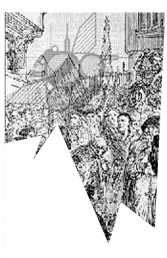

Robert Aske's rebellion found sympathizers all over England.

This is the gravestone of Robert Kett, leader of the rebellion in Norfolk.

▶ **Source: Sir Thomas Smith, A Discourse of the Commonweal of this Realm of England, 1549**
Sir Thomas Smith wrote about the enclosures:

"These enclosures ... make us pay dearer for our land that we occupy... where forty persons had their livings, now one man and his shepherd hath all."

THE PILGRIMAGE OF GRACE

The 1536 Pilgrimage of Grace was a rebellion that started in Lincolnshire and Yorkshire because of Henry VIII's anti-Catholic changes. The rebels wanted the king to stop closing the monasteries. The rebel leader was a lawyer called Robert Aske.

▶ **Source: Edward Hall, Chronicles, 1542**

Edward Hall described the rebellion:

> "They called this … a holy and blessed pilgrimage; they also had certain banners … whereon was painted Christ hanging on the cross …"

Eventually about 30,000 rebels joined the rebellion. Henry VIII pretended to negotiate but RENEGED on his promises. The leaders of the rebellion were executed. Robert Aske was burned at the stake.

Words to use in your project

clergy – *people ordained for religious service*
concession – *a grant or the act of giving in*
plot – *a secret, usually evil, project or scheme*
populist – *a supporter of the rights and power of the common people*
stratum – *a division of society (plural: strata)*

Glossary

confessed – *admitted to being guilty*
execution – *the act of putting someone to death*
rebellions – *acts of resistance to an established government or ruler*
rebels – *the people involved in a rebellion*
reneged – *go back on your word*
revolt – *a rising up against the government*

See also: The Tudors 4–5; Religion 10–11; Buildings 16–17; Crime and Punishment 24–25

CASE STUDY

Anne Askew

Anne Askew was a Protestant who married a Catholic. Anne went to London to distribute banned Protestant booklets and her husband was ordered to take her home – but she escaped. This time she was taken to the Tower of London and tortured to give the names of other Protestants.

▶ **Source: Diary of Anne Askew, 1546**

Here she describes what happened:

> "… they did put me on the rack, because I CONFESSED no ladies or gentlemen, to be of my opinion … the Lord Chancellor and Master Rich took pains to rack me with their own hands, till I was nearly dead … I said that I would rather die than break my faith."

A 16th-century engraving showing the EXECUTION of Anne Askew and others.

Tudor Towns

Life in the towns of England changed dramatically during the Tudor period because of increased TRADE. A new merchant class emerged and moved to good trading areas, including the River Thames in London, where ships full of goods could dock. The towns and cities were dirty, smelly and dangerous, with open sewers and gangs of robbers.

LIFE AROUND LONDON

Sir Thomas Gresham was a Tudor merchant.

When Henry VII became king, the population of London was about 75,000, but by 1600 it had risen to 200,000. The Tudors established London as the centre for trade and government. It was a lively, bustling place with merchants and traders selling their wares on the street. Craftsmen and traders specializing in certain goods often established themselves in the same street. Today all that remains are the names.

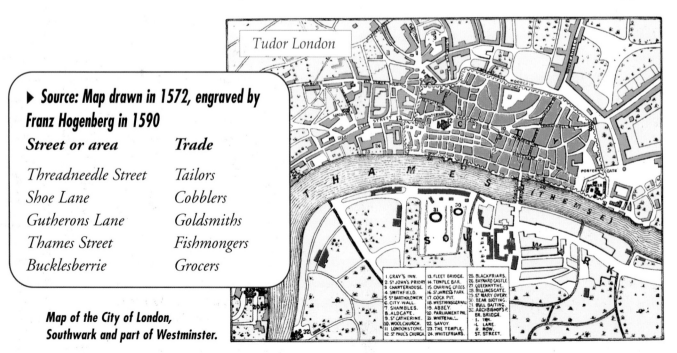

Tudor London

▶ **Source: Map drawn in 1572, engraved by Franz Hogenberg in 1590**

Street or area	Trade
Threadneedle Street	Tailors
Shoe Lane	Cobblers
Gutherons Lane	Goldsmiths
Thames Street	Fishmongers
Bucklesberrie	Grocers

Map of the City of London, Southwark and part of Westminster.

MARKET AND TRADE

The wool trade had a significant effect on Tudor life, and many market towns specialized in selling sheep and their fleeces. West of London, the towns of Reading, Abingdon and Newbury were centres for the cloth trade.

> ▶ **Source: Excerpt from the diary of Swiss traveller Thomas Platter, who came to London in 1599**
>
> Thomas Platter gives an account of London merchants:
>
> *"They buy, sell and trade in all the corners of the globe … There are also many wealthy merchants, moneychangers and bankers in this city. Some of them sell expensive goods, while others deal only in money or wholesale goods."*

Markets also flourished. At markets local craftsmen, PEDLARS, grain merchants, fruit sellers, fishmongers and BUTCHERS sold their produce. As well as traders, there were rogues, VAGABONDS, QUACKS, fortune-tellers, tumblers, dancers and other entertainers.

Words to use in your project

demography – *the statistical science of human populations*
entrepreneur – *a risk taker, especially in business*
infrastructure – *a basic framework*
migrate – *to leave one's country and settle in another*
suburb – *a residential district outside a city*

Glossary

butchers – *people who prepare and sell meat*
pedlars – *sellers of small goods*
quacks – *untrained people who pretend to be physicians*
trade – *the buying, selling and bartering of goods*
vagabonds – *homeless people*

See also: Marriage and Family 8–9; Buildings 16–17; Art 20–21; Crime and Punishment 24–25; Sports and Pastimes 30–31

CASE STUDY

The curfew bell

The curfew was a way of making sure people did not leave their homes after dark. During this time there was no police force and no street lighting, so criminals could go undetected. As well as the curfew, towns also closed city gates to protect citizens. There was so much political unrest that the Tudor monarchs did not want people to be able to meet secretly after nightfall. The curfew was sounded by the local church bell.

This curfew bell hung from the Tower of London.

Sports and Pastimes

Tudor people enjoyed many pastimes, including board games, GAMBLING and hunting. For royalty and the nobility, JOUSTING TOURNAMENTS were favourite events. Some Tudor sports, including BEAR-BAITING and cockfighting, are now illegal.

GAMES PLAYED

Football during Tudor times was a violent game. By 1540 it had become so dangerous that Henry VIII banned it.

> ▶ **Source: Philip Stubbes, The Anatomie of Abuses, 1585**
> The following account by Philip Stubbes describes how brutal football was:
>
> *"Football playing ... may rather be called a friendly kind of fight than a play for recreation, a bloody and MURTHERING practice than a felowly sport."*

In 1512, Henry VIII passed a law that banned ordinary people from playing almost all sports, except archery. This was partly because he needed archers for his royal army. At Christmas time the law was relaxed so that people could enjoy themselves. Kings and members of the nobility loved hunting and only they were allowed to hunt deer.

Only royals and nobles were allowed to hunt deer and STAGS, like this one.

ROYAL TOURNAMENTS

Only the king and members of the nobility could take part in a Tudor royal tournament. Jousting was the most spectacular event.

Elaborate **ARMOUR** was used during tournaments.

> ▶ **Source: An account written by George Cavendish, Duke of Surrey, 1524**

Henry VIII was an accomplished jouster, but suffered a bad injury when jousting with the Duke of Surrey, as this account by George Cavendish explains:

"… the duke set forward and charged with his spear, and the king likewise unadvisedly set off towards the duke. The people, seeing the king's face bare, cried hold, hold … Alas, what sorrow was it to the people when they saw the splinters of the duke's spear strike the king's headpiece."

Words to use in your project

competition – *a contest*
discriminate – *to make distinctions*
elite – *a group regarded as the finest*
fatal – *resulting in death*
gruesome – *causing horror*
leisure – *free time*
outdoors – *outside*

Glossary

armour – *a metal covering worn to protect the body against weapons*
bear-baiting – *a form of entertainment in which dogs are encouraged to torment a chained bear*
gambling – *games of chance played for money*
jousting – *a sport in which knights on horseback fight using lances*
lance – *a long wooden shaft with a sharp, pointed metal head*
murthering – *the old spelling of 'murdering'*
stags – *full-grown male deer*
tournaments – *sporting competitions*

See also: The Tudors 4–5; Religion 10–11; Crime and Punishment 24–25

CA

J

> ▶ **Source: An account by Luis Caroz, court ambassador, 1510**

In 1510, the Spanish ambassador Luis Caroz wrote:

"There are many young men who excel in this kind of warfare, but the most conspicuous among them all, the most interested in the combats is the King himself, who never omits being present at them."

Jousting developed as a way for knights to practise fighting.

Index

A
actors 18
archery 30
architecture 16, 20
artists 14, 20
Askew, Anne 27
B
banquets 23
Boleyn, Anne 7, 10
C
cargo 15
Catholics 10
children 8, 9, 22
Church of England 6, 10, 15
classes (society) 5, 12, 17, 18, 22, 23, 28
clothes 12
composers 21
costume 18
courts (law) 25
crime 24
Cromwell, Thomas 11, 15
curfew 2

D
Drake, Sir Francis 15
E
Elizabeth I 7, 8, 11, 13, 14, 15, 18, 19, 20, 21
entertainers 2
F
fashion 12, 13
food 9, 22–3
football 30
G
Globe Theatre 19
Gresham, Thomas 28
H
Hampton Court Palace 17
Hardwick Hall 16
Henry VII 4, 6, 10, 14, 17, 25, 28
Henry VIII 5, 6, 7, 8, 9, 11, 14, 15, 16, 20, 21, 26, 27, 30, 31
Hilliard, Nicholas 21
Holbein, Hans 20
houses 16
hunting 30

J
jewellery 12, 21
jousting 31
justice 24
Justices of the Peace 25
L
laws 12, 24, 25
London 28
Longleat House 16
M
markets 29
merchants 5, 22, 28, 29
monasteries 6, 11, 26
money 6, 9
monks 11
music 21
P
painting 20–1
palaces 17
peasants 5, 26
plays 18, 19
Pope 10
population (London) 28

portraits 20–1
Protestants 10, 11
punishments 12, 24, 25, 26
R
Raleigh, Sir Walter 14
rebellions 26–27
royalty 30
S
Shakespeare, William 14, 19
spices 23
sports 30
T
Teerline, Lavinia 21
thatched roofs 16
theatres 18–19
tournaments 30, 31
Tower of London 24, 27, 29
trade 7, 13, 28, 29
W
Wars of the Roses 4, 5
weddings 8
witchcraft 24
wives of Henry VIII 7
Wolsey, Thomas 14, 15, 17

Tudor Timeline

1486

Henry VII (Tudor) marries Elizabeth of York uniting the houses of York and Lancaster.

1509

Henry VIII succeeds Henry VII as king.

1515

Thomas Wolsey, Archbishop of York, is made Lord Chancellor of England and cardinal.

1521

Henry VIII receives the title 'Defender of the Faith' from Pope Leo X for his opposition to Protestant Martin Luther.

1529

Henry VIII dismisses Lord Chancellor Thomas Wolsey for failing to obtain the Pope's consent to his divorce from Catherine of Aragon.

1533

Henry VIII marries Anne Boleyn and is excommunicated by Pope Clement VII; new Protestant Church of England created.

1553

Lady Jane Grey becomes queen for nine days. Her successor is Mary Tudor.

1558

Elizabeth I becomes queen. Spanish Armada sea battle takes place.

1564

William Shakespeare is born in Stratford-upon-Avon.

1577

Sir Francis Drake sets off in Golden Hind to circumnavigate the globe.

1587

Execution of Mary Queen of Scots; England at war with Spain.

1603

Elizabeth I dies. The Tudor era comes to an end. James VI of Scotland becomes James I of England and the Stewart era begins.